THE BEGI GUIDE TO

The Ultimate Guide To MMA Training For Newbies

So you're thinking of taking up MMA, mixed martial arts. The first question you have to ask yourself is, why? I'm serious, defining what you want to accomplish is an important first step in finding and staying with a training regimen that will meet the ultimate goals you have for yourself and MMA.

Is your goal to compete in UFC style competitions? Do you want to learn to defend yourself? Are you looking for a serious workout for improved physical fitness? Your goals are your own, but honestly answering the previous questions and knowing what you want to achieve are tantamount for finding the right kind of program and one that will ultimately meet all your needs and be able to fulfill your goals. The following article should help answer these questions and help you make the best decisions without having to fumble around and lose precious time doing the research yourself.

MMA, A Brief History

I believe it's important to understand the history of any undertaking to understand where you belong in the grand scheme of things. With any passion you might have, it's important to know where it came from and where it's going.

MMA originally existed in the Classic Greek era of the Olympic Games. The sport of Pankration, which combined grappling and striking skills, was a great deal like the modern mixed martial arts. This form of fighting was passed on to the Romans and later morphed into Greco-Roman wrestling, which morphed again into the modern Olympic style wrestling we have today.

Modern MMA is believed to be a culmination of fighting skills that looked to identify the best unarmed martial art style and vale tudo in Brazil and *Tough Guy Contests* in the United States were early forerunners to the fighting contests we see in the UFC and StrikeForce. These modern organizations, which feature MMA fighting, are the reason the sport has caught back on in the past two decades. Modern MMA uses an assortment of fighting and martial art disciplines to train fighters for self-defense and competition. The beauty of MMA is that you don't have to excel at one style of fighting. Well rounded fighters, who have good skills in a multitude of styles, are usually better fighters then someone who trains in just boxing or karate. One of the best aspects of learning MMA is that you are exposed to many different styles and you get to choose which one's fit best with your particular skill set.

Where Do I Begin?

There is no hard and fast rule about where to begin your training journey. A big part of where to begin can be found in the answers to the questions from earlier about why you want to train and what do you want to accomplish. My advice is to go watch some old UFC fights on YouTube. Rent past episodes of The Ultimate Fighter reality TV series. This is a peek into the life of professionally trained fighters looking to make it into the UFC. It will show you the commitment it takes to train and compete in MMA as a professional fighter. This is the most extreme of the goals of taking up MMA and as with any professional sport, only a few make it to the top. If this is your goal, you will need to evaluate every aspect of your life and understand that you are making a commitment that will be full of trials and tribulations. To become an MMA professional, you must consider moving to a large city or finding a gym that has a training club, specifically designed to train MMA professionals.

Before starting on any training, no matter what you have as an ultimate goal, you must go to your Dr. and get a physical. Inform the doctor of your goal of competing in MMA and let him know what you expect to get out of your training. The doctor can look for and identify possible issues, evaluate what your current fitness level, and give recommendations as to what level of exercise you should start. The best kind of doctor to go to would be a sports medicine specialist.

Find a Gym and Trainer

MMA has become big business in recent history. From ex-athletes looking to re-enter the competitive life to people wanting a serious workout regimen, most gyms offer some sort of MMA type training. This fact allows for any number of con artists and thieves to prey on people who want to be trained in MMA. The internet and client interviews are your best bet to finding and retaining a reliable, competent instructor.

Your first visit should be the internet. Search for "MMA Trainers and Instructors". Compile a list of 4 to 5 names that meet the type of training in which you want to participate. The trainer is the most important aspect to search for, because they will be doing the actual teaching. Once you have identified the prospective trainers, type their names in Google to see if they have any bad press against them. A word of caution, don't make this the only qualifier, some people may have a grudge against a person, who is an otherwise good trainer, but since it's so easy to use the internet to sully a person's reputation, an opportunity might be missed if you go solely on this initial internet search.

Look for an instructor that has well rounded experience. In most cases, you will have to go to 2-3 instructors to learn all the aspects of MMA, but a good instructor is one that has actually competed and trained in MMA. You can look on certification sites to see if your potential instructor has been certified, this will increase the chances of finding a competent trainer. These sites include: mmainstructorcertification.org, National Academy of Sports Medicine-nasm.org, American Sports and Fitness Association-asfa.org.

Finally, ask your potential instructor for personal references. Ask him to give you 2 or 3 references and if possible an ex-client. Most instructors won't have a problem with this and should have these readily available. Finally, sit in on a few of their classes, both experienced and beginner. This will allow you to experience the expectations of the class before you actually attend. If the particular class doesn't look like what you want of if there seems to be a lack of people your age and size, select another class.

 It's probably best to have 2 or 3 selections to choose from and it's important to go check out every one of them to see which one will best fit your schedule and offer you the best options for partners. If there isn't more than one option in your town, ask a buddy to come along and be your partner. This will help keep you committed if you have someone else depending on you to attend and it can take the anxiety out of the first days of class when you are learning the ins and outs of the instructor and course. MMA is also something your entire family can do together. Have your wife and children over 12 years old participate in the class with you, or at least have them come watch on days you know you will be sparring. This will help to keep you motivated by showing how much you have learned and will give your family confidence in you as a protector. The same goes for wives inviting their husbands. Family involvement can be key to staying with the program.

Format a Training Plan

Your instructor should have a program that will outline your training week by week. It should cover which area of martial arts you will learn, what additional training you will be required to perform, such as strength training and aerobic exercise. Your workouts should be broken down into categories and a schedule established. Most instructors will have classes that have a set time. They should offer beginning, intermediate and advanced class or classes. Do your best to attend the same class at the same time for the first two months, this will allow you to become comfortable and familiar with the training process.

The instructor should also have a list of equipment you will need to bring with you. Most common are workout clothes, t-shirts and shorts or sweats, sparring gloves and/or hand wraps, mouth guards, athletic supporters (jock straps), sports bras for women, and tennis shoes, although most MMA training is done in bare feet, your class may be required to run or lift weights, both of which require trainers or tennis shoes. Make sure you ask your instructor if there is any special equipment you will need.

Different Disciplines in MMA

It's important to know what type of fighting styles, or disciplines there are in MMA. No one person can be proficient in all styles and most instructors will be proficient in training you for 3 or 4 different styles. A world class gym, like Jackson-Winkeljohn MMA in Albuquerque, NM will teach several different disciplines but limits fighters who compete professionally to certain styles that complement each other. Modern MMA will have different aspects that are universal and come from different styles. For example, striking, comes from American boxing, Muay Thai, and other hand offensive styles. Grappling can encompass Brazilian Jiu-Jitsu, freestyle and catch wrestling or even Sambo.

It is important to know the different styles of fighting and what the basis for each style covers. Below is a list of the most common fighting styles in MMA and what major discipline they cover.

Brazilian Jiu-Jitsu (BJJ)

Ground fighting art concerned with joint locks, strangulations, submissions and control from back. Made popular by Royce Gracie

Freestyle and Greco-Roman Wrestling

Amateur wrestling style practiced in the Olympic Games. Combines takedowns with ground fighting and submissions

Sambo

Russian form of Judo mixed with strikes and wrestling

Aikido

Japanese style of fighting mixing Jujitsu and Kenjutsu. Uses opponent's motion against him. Takes attackers motion and uses it to disable and submit attacker. Morihei Ueshiba is the developer of this style.

Boxing
American form of boxing

Muay Thai
Thailand fighting that combines punching with leg strikes, knees, elbows and high kicks for offense.

There are many more forms of fighting and different gyms will teach different styles. These are the more popular ones done in today's MMA, but there are many more I didn't cover. Check with your instructor or gym to find out which one's on which you will be focusing. Some people take easier to one style over another, but the goal of MMA is to challenge yourself. If you find one style more appealing than another, you may be able to follow up and take training specifically for that style.

Attend Your First Class

Nothing is as nerve racking and exciting as your first class. Make sure you go in as relaxed as possible, don't try to overdo it or show off in any way. Everyone starts somewhere and no one expects you to be John Jones your first day of training. Make sure you warm up and stretch properly before starting the training. If something doesn't make sense of if you are having trouble with a move, ask questions now, don't wait and try to fake your way through it. Most martial arts are built on fundamental skills and if you miss one, then the next will be harder to master.

A good practice session should consist of the following:

Warm Up
The Warm Up consists of stretching and using movement to warm up the body slowly. (10-15 minutes)
Technique and Drilling
Learning a move or kick from a martial art style and then doing that move against an opponent. Usually done at half speed and done as perfectly as possible. (20-40 minutes)
Sparring
Actual fighting at ¾ to full speed, this is your opportunity to try the techniques you are learning in a faster environment. Can also be full out competition. This is where you should try newly learned moves and take chances. (20-30 minutes)
Conditioning

This is where you build up stamina for real competition. Should be some sort of anaerobic exercise coupled with biking, running long distance or circuit training. (20-30 minutes)

These can be mixed around except for the warm up cycle, which should always be done first.

Important Aspects for Training

When training your body there are many aspects that a person should keep in mind. The first is proper diet. Depending on your level of training, diet can play a huge role in how well you perform and how your body responds to the intense training involved in MMA.

There are several different diet plans out on the market and I won't recommend a specific plan over another. I will suggest that you increase your caloric intake to match what you are putting out and to balance your diet with proteins, carbohydrates and fat. The American Heart Association has a good example of a balanced diet, just increase the amounts for calories taken in to what you are spending. A good diet will help maintain energy levels, rebuild muscle and keep you going during long training sessions. It also helps to balance blood sugar and body chemistry. Make sure you find and keep a good diet during training and even consider making it a lifestyle change. MMA competitions are done by weight and you are going to want to find and maintain a weight that feels comfortable and where you don't have to "cut" a lot of weight if you decide to compete. Your body will adjust after a few months of training and you can judge at what weight you would like to compete.

Weight classes can differ among the different organizations but most of them follow this system of weight classes.

Flyweight—125 lbs. or 56.7kg
Bantamweight—135 lbs. or 61.2 kg
Featherweight—145 lbs. or 65.8 kg
Lightweight—155 lbs. or 70.3 kg
Welterweight—170 lbs. or 77.1 kg
Middleweight—185 lbs. or 83.9 kg
Light Heavyweight—205 lbs. or 93 kg
Heavyweight—265 lbs. or 120 kg
Super Heavyweight—No weight limit

Knowing what weight class you want to compete in is important and your goal should be to stay within 5 pounds of that weight before competition. If you have trouble making your weight it may be better to build muscle and go to the next weight class. Cutting large amounts of weight before a competition can make you weak and take focus from concentrating on the fight. This will also help you size up your partners for training. You don't want to fight to far above or below your class.

Recovery from exercise is as important as the exercise itself. If you don't give your body time to recover and let muscles rebuild, you will fatigue quickly and you won't see gains like you should. The best way to balance recovery to exercise is to start off with a balanced week of one day of exercise to one day of rest. This will let your body get used to the physical changes that take place when you begin exercising more heavily. You can increase the days of exercise as you build stamina and energy, but don't overdo it, your body has to have some rest to rebuild. Also, rest means sleep also. It is recommended while training to get a solid 8 hours of sleep each night. Treat your training schedule like an Olympic athlete does, train while your training, don't go out and party on your off nights or on the weekend. You are trying to achieve something here and overeating, not sleeping and partying can undo all your hard work.

Other Training Options

Besides the training you will receive in an instructor lead class, you may also want to consider some other forms of training that can complement your classroom learning.

Because MMA is an anaerobic sport in which you have bursts of motion mixed with periods of rest, you want to build other aspects of your body to round out your training. Biking or running distance are great ways to build your lung capacity and train your muscles to last longer. In a true fight, your muscles will burn out, especially if you hold your opponent in a position that requires you to exert muscle control for a long period of time. These exercises, or any that train your muscles to work for long periods of time, will help you when you need that extra push to submit your opponent or make it through the end of a long training class.

Strength training may also assist you as you train for MMA. Building muscle can assist you in delivering more forceful strikes and kicks, help you build muscle to assist in submission holds and can tone your muscles to build longevity. Fatigue is one of the MMA fighter's worst enemies and any supplemental exercises you can do will help increase your stamina. Follow an approved MMA strength training course that helps build the muscles that will be needed in MMA. Also, make sure your instructor is part of your training plan as you go forward. Let them know what you plan to do as far as alternative training and what program you plan to follow. Most instructors won't have an issue with you doing work on your own but they need to be a part of the planning process. The key to any training is not to overdo it. Your body needs time to rest and recover and you don't want to subvert that by working out like a maniac.

Other good training options to assist you in MMA are ballet, gymnastics, parkour, and dance class. These can help you with footwork and developing a sense of balance and athleticism.

Who Can Train in MMA?

I believe that anyone who wants to learn to defend themselves to those who want to be in incredible physical shape should consider training in MMA. It is a great sport for people of all ages and sexes and no one that is physically able, should discount MMA training. Some think that women shouldn't be allowed to compete because of the violent nature of the sport, but for those naysayers I would point out Rhonda Rousey. She is an incredibly tough and high spirited competitor who would beat many of the men competing at the same weight. I have also seen Randy Couture, a former UFC heavy weight champion, compete professionally up to his 50th birthday. So the only limitation is those we would set on ourselves.

I don't want to make anyone believe they can take up MMA at any age. It is a tough sport and can really work over your joints and muscles. I can't stress enough that a person needs to seek medical advice before beginning MMA workouts and if you have pre-existing medical issues, like a bad back, it's probably wise to stay away from the fighting/sparring aspects of MMA. The technique and drilling will probably be ok for the older person, but make sure you clear that with your doctor.

There are MMA classes for seniors and more kid's classes are being offered. It's best to find one of these classes for kids under 13 years old and for seniors over 55. These classes will concentrate heavily on drilling and technique and probably won't have much if any actual sparring. These classes are good for older people wanting to learn self-defense and kids who want to begin learning MMA in a safe environment.

Philosophical Advice

In order to prosper and excel in a sport like MMA, you need to learn some philosophy of fighting. There are physical and psychological techniques that will make you a better fighter and should be practiced at every opportunity.

Train for Pain

MMA requires a great personal sacrifice. It can lead to difficult physical demands and the nature of the game requires living with and enduring pain. Don't half ass your training and think that you can compete. Even sparring in the practice room can be painful and you need to prepare yourself mentally to be able to take that pain. You need to train in techniques that teach you to take a punch or absorb a kick. You need to learn to land and fall correctly and most importantly, you need to learn when to TAP OUT. Too many people mistake pride for bravery and can get injured by trying to endure something the human body shouldn't endure, tapping out is the process of submission by tapping your opponent or the ring's mat to say you have had enough or that you give up. There is no dishonor in tapping out, it's far better to tap out then to lose half a year training because of a torn shoulder or knee.

Learn to Breath

Because MMA is an anaerobic sport, we have a tendency to hold our breath as we strain in combat. When we are engaged in a flurry of offense, we instinctually hold our breath, that is why we tire out so quickly and why we have to "take a break" between offensive moves. We need to learn to keep breathing when we attack. Breathe out on a punch or kick with a sharp quick breath from the diaphragm. This helps keep your muscles tense for defending attacks from your opponent. Focus on breathing when sparring so that when you compete it is more natural to breathe appropriately.

Focus on Longevity and Persistence

MMA is a huge commitment. The amount of time we give to the training and the amount of sacrifice we give to learn these techniques would make it seem obvious that we want to be in MMA for a long time. We don't want to suffer an injury or give up because we aren't improving as well as we should. MMA should be seen as a long journey over time and not a short trip that's over quickly. You will experience times where you are learning and improving with some ease and then there will be times when your hit a plateau and your progress seems to almost stop. Remember, we are in this for the long term and highs and lows are to be expected. Don't give up at the smallest speed bump, we need to train like we are going to be around for the next 20 years.

Sparring VS. Drilling

You can find a huge difference of opinion on this subject but most reputable trainers agree that drilling should be given more time and focus than sparring. In order to learn a new technique, like a new leg kick or how to throw a jab, we need to do that move over 1000 times in a perfect controlled manner. This allows our muscles to build up "memory" and when we need to do it in a bout, the muscle and brain will execute it like we practiced it. We only do this type of practice during our drilling cycle. Sparring is when we get to try it out in the real world in a full out combat exercise. It's the same reason a sniper shoots thousands of rounds at a paper target each week, so that when they have to make the "kill" shot in real life, they are ready. Another theory about drilling is to "mentally" drill whenever possible. We need to visualize ourselves performing the technique perfectly in our imaginations several times each night before bed, or every morning when we wake up. This is said to "trick" our bodies into performing the technique perfectly in a sparring or competition bout.

Why Study MMA?

This might be a good time to re-evaluate why we want to do MMA. After you have been to a month's worth of classes and have had the opportunity to spar, we need to ask ourselves the question we asked in the beginning, "Why do I want to do MMA?" MMA can be a good source of physical exercise, a way to learn self-defense, or a start to some level of competition within the MMA professional fight world. The best time to answer this question is after you have done the workouts for about a month.

After a month you should know if your original goal is worth pursuing or if you need to change your original thoughts into something more. MMA is first and foremost, a great physical workout. If you want nothing more than to improve your body, lose weight, and tone your muscles, MMA can help tremendously in these areas.

MMA is also a great way to improve your self-defense awareness. It teaches a variety of martial art and grappling disciplines that will assist you in the real world if you are attacked and want to fight back. The technique portion of your workouts are especially helpful here and you should take great care in relating what you are learning in class to how it can help you in a real world mugging. This is true for both men and women. MMA is a great way for women to learn to not only defend themselves, but also to go on the offensive and disable their attacker. It can do wonders for your self-esteem and confidence in these regards. MMA will make you more confident because you are better able to handle yourself if things get rough. A bit of caution here though, MMA isn't to be used as a source to bully someone or to go out and beat up people for kicks. As a trained MMA fighter you are subject to laws that can classify you as a lethal weapon and you may be prosecuted more harshly for fighting without provocation.

Finally, for the person who decides they want to try their hand at competition, MMA is the fastest growing competitive professional sport in the United States. Local competitions can be found on a monthly basis and in your region you will be able to support yourself fairly well as you train and gain experience. It can take several years and some luck to make it to the big time with MMA fighting and for many it never happens. You need to decide how far you want to go and how much you are willing to give up to decide to go full professional. This will most likely require going to a city and finding a gym like Jackson MMA to take you on as a fighter.

Leave your Ego at the Door

You are not John Jones or Rhonda Rousey, yet. You are not the greatest MMA fighter ever unleashed, yet. Someday you may become these things or eclipse these people, but for now you are you. A beginner looking to improve yourself. Don't let early success or a natural ability go to your head. There is always someone out there who can beat you. Just ask John Jones or Anderson Silva. Be humble and gracious in victory and defeat. Don't try to watch a UFC fight one weekend then go see if you can replicate the flying back kick you saw Anderson Silva throw on Nate Diaz. You aren't a MMA professional and most of the upper level fighters have trained for years to be able to perform the amazing strikes and kicks you see on pay-per-view fights.

Beginner Sparring Tips

Sparring is an important aspect of your training. It can help you judge the progress you are making, find and work on weaknesses you might have, and ultimately give you some real world experience in what it feels like to actually fight in a real match. Sparring is usually not full out fighting, although you want a class that allows full speed sparring at least once a month. Mostly sparring is a ¾ speed bout that will allow you to work on the techniques you have learned and see if you can perform them in a live fight. Sparring should be about ¼ of your training time and should not be the main focus of what you do in a practice. Make sure and partner with people who are the same skill level or a little better than you. This will keep things interesting and won't give you a false sense of overconfidence. Be honest with yourself about your skill level and don't sandbag yourself when picking a partner.

Partner Up—Find a partner whose skill level is even or a little better than your own. Sparring with people who don't challenge you will discourage you or give you a false sense that you are better than you really are.

Use New Techniques—Challenge yourself to try out the new kicks or strikes that you learned this week. Don't keep using techniques you know you are good at, but make yourself work on your weaknesses. Sparring should be used to improve your skill and only by trying new skills can we get better.

Be aggressive— if you are usually a defensive fighter, make yourself be aggressive. Change up your fighting style to go on an offensive against your opponent. You may need it when you're losing in a real bout and you need to do something to win.

Practice Like You Are in a Real Bout—unless the instructor has ordered you to go ½ or ¾ speed, spar like you are in a real MMA fight. We generally perform like we practice so it's important to make every full speed spar seem like a real live fight.

Take Chances—Take chances on different moves and techniques. If you normally don't leg strike, make yourself leg strike. If your stand up is weak, make yourself stay on your feet and be aggressive. If you don't take chances in a sparring match you won't take them in a real match.

Some Basic Effective Techniques for MMA

Have you ever wondered what the most popular and powerful MMA techniques are? Here's our list of the top submissions taught in MMA gyms all over the world.

WARNING: not all of these techniques are legal in competition, or allowed at all gyms. But it's still better to be familiar with these illegal techniques just in case someone tries to use them on you. And many of these illegal MMA moves still have a ton of validity for MMA applications or self defense situations, so they are well worth learning!

1. Guillotine Choke

The gullotine choke is a major submission move that is regularly applied when you're standing or in the closed guard position. There are numerous variations of the Choke, including the Marcelotine, the Arm- in and the 10 Finger choke.

How to perform this move:
a) **Bend your opponent over.**
   Snap their head down. The point is to get their head down to your chest.

b) **Wrap your arm around the neck.**
   Their neck has to be set between your lower arm and bicep.

c) **Pull your opponent's neck down to your hip and arm.**
   This will put a lot of weight on their neck.

d) If your opponent tries to take you down to the ground, wrap your legs around their body as soon as you touch the ground.

e) **Keep applying similar pressure as a sleeper hold.**
This will either incapacitate them or force a tap out.

Videos of the Gullotine Choke
Marcelotine: https://youtu.be/2ortF7sjrrc
Guillotine from Closed Guard: https://youtu.be/DLrXGWLtOoU
Standing Guillotine: https://youtu.be/nCCVE3zQfqc
Arm-in Guillotine Choke: https://youtu.be/QQQpUM8Q2os

2. Rear Naked Choke

The Rear Naked Choke is also called the sleeper hold, which is one of the most critical submissions in MMA. This move is the most elegant approach to end a fight.

How to perform this move:

a) **Get behind your opponent and drop them to the ground.**
The rear naked choke, as the name suggests, makes it necessary that you are behind your opponent. While the hold can also be performed from the standing position, it is recommended to drop your opponent to the ground for better control and a better chance of finishing the submission.

b) **Wrap your legs around them, so that your insteps are within their thighs or knees.**
At the same time, put one arm over their neck and towards the focal point of the chest, while placing your other arm under your opponent's. Fasten your hands together in a tight grasp over the chest in what is known as the seat belt.

c) **Release the seat belt and put one arm around your opponent's neck.**
This would probably be the upper arm of the seat belt position but it doesn't make any difference. Attempt to get your elbow against thier chin, so that the throat

is on the inside of your elbow. The arm around the opponent's neck will consequently be referred to as your "main hand", while the free arm is dubbed as your "off hand".

d) **Use your main hand to grab the bicep of the off hand.**
The grasp is frequently called as the "figure four", because of the way your arms shape the number 4 when performing it. This can serve as a rule in case you are uncertain on how you ought to hold your opponent.

e) **Keep the figure-four hold in place.**
Place your off hand of the moment against the back of your opponent's neck, to the point where it's attached to the arm that is circled around the neck. For reasons that will be examined below, it is advisable that you make a fist, as it won't be grabbing anything for the rest of the hold.

f) **Squeeze.**
Gradually, flex the arm that is choking as much as you can, while pushing your off hand into your opponent's neck from behind. If the choke is executed properly, it will interrupt the blood stream to the brain, bringing about unconsciousness in just about 4 to 5 seconds.

Videos of the Rear Naked Choke
Basic RNC: https://youtu.be/176SLdBhj_A
RNC Trick: https://youtu.be/-ciTiubaFa8
RNC – The most common errors: https://youtu.be/K5IVkWszO8U
Bas Rutten's RNC: https://youtu.be/LppnEfRoFIM

3. Triangle Choke

The Triangle Choke is a signature move in grappling and it has brought a lot of sparring sessions and matches to an end. The Triangle Choke can be a difficult submission move and it can take a while to master the finer points that make this choke so effective. Be that as it may, if you have long and flexible legs, then this may very well be your signature move.

How to perform this move:
a. **Begin by laying on your back with your legs separated.**
Your opponent's waist should be in the middle of your legs. This is called "open guard" as their movements are somewhat limited by your legs but not as much as they would be if your legs were wrapped around his middle or in the "closed guard" position.

b) At this time, as your opponent is caught inside your guard, they will be attempting to use their elbows while searching for a way to break your guard. To start setting up your triangle choke you need to get one of the arms as they are attempting to open your guard and divert it so it moves to the side of your head instead of hitting it. Once this is achieved you should make every effort to hold the now extended arm locked in this position.

c) **Pull yourself into position.**
When your opponent's attack has been diverted and their arm is locked it is time to position your own body. You do this by using your legs to push your body so that your opponent is far from your head. With some practice you ought to have the capacity to position your body at the same time as protecting yourself from any manoeuvring attempts or attacks from the remaining arm.

d) **Pivot your hips forward.**
This will force your opponent's body to slide further down yours.

e) You now need to figure out how to manoeuvre one of your legs over the arm of your opponent that was pushed down and far from you.

f) **Begin to raise your legs above and over your opponent's head.**
At this time you should be in a position where your opponent's head is between your hips. You should also still maintain a firm hold of their arm at the side of your head. It's time to begin raising your legs up and over your opponents head. You need to start wrapping one leg around your opponent's head and shoulders making constantly sure that their arm is still caught between their own neck and head. Bring your foot towards your other leg.

g) **Wrap your knee around the feet of your other leg securing your opponent's immobilization.**
Use your shin to position your leg over your opponent's back to facilitate the choke, but do not put pressure on your foot as this can cause you to break your shin or dislocate your ankle.

h) **Using your legs you need to apply as much pressure as you can to the neck and head of your opponent.**
You will notice that gradually your opponent's arm that is locked against the neck limits the airflow to the lungs of your opponent. You can use one of your hands to pull down on the head which will apply significantly more pressure which will bring faster tap for the choke.

i) Hold the choke until your opponent either taps out, the referee stops the battle, or your opponent is incapacitated.

Videos of Triangle Chokes
Basic Triangle Choke: https://youtu.be/IwN-E7LO3bM
5 Triangle Chokes you must know: https://youtu.be/FbXunEbkf8E
Triangle Choke Mount: https://youtu.be/gc5YRdv-wSw
The 4 most common errors: https://youtu.be/9yfi5N1O3dA

4. Kimura / Keylock

The Kimura is an effective arm lock that is performed against your opponent's arm at the level of their chest and in front, focusing on the shoulder and elbow joints.

How to perform this grip:

a) Take your opponent in the closed guard position.

b) To break their stance pull their body into yours with your legs as you use your hands to push their arms out to the side.

c) Now grab their right wrist with your left hand, open your feet, and sit up toward that arm to secure it into the Kimura position (wrapping around your opponent's arm with your right arm and grabbing your own wrist).

d) To complete the grip, lie back to the floor and move into your opponent while pushing their hips away. Put your right foot to their left side hip, through your left leg high above their upper back, and get the submission.

Videos of the Kimura
Traditional Kimura: https://youtu.be/HA-2NRuTLkw
Kimura from Guard: https://youtu.be/xqSdVL82QVk
Kimura from Side Control: https://youtu.be/QT0TqceznpQ
Kimura - 3 Most Common Errors: https://youtu.be/nJotiTewRbI

Standing Kimura: https://youtu.be/SnLuzJi23MA
Sakuraba style Kimuras: https://youtu.be/Ly11uw2l-8o

5. Ude Garami (aka Americana / V Armlock)

This technique is one of the first ones you learn in most grappling arts. It is a twisting grip that most of the time focuses on the shoulder joint, resulting in a submission, a bone break, or a dislocation .

How to execute:
a) Put your opponent on his back. Hold your opponent's lower arm with both hands so his wrist is twisted upwards and facing outwards.

b) Position your legs so that your knees are twisted in such a way that your opponent's arm and elbow is positioned between your legs.

c) Kick both of your feet upwards while pulling on his arm to draw both bodies while keeping the arm positioned wrist up. The outcome should be to find your groin under or near your opponent's shoulder.

d) Wrap both legs over his chest (one on every side of the arm) while maintaining their elbow straight to force their wrist towards you.

e) Using your opponent's chest as support, pull their wrist towards your chest and apply upward pressure using your hips. It won't take long before the technique compels your opponent to tap out.

Videos of the Americana:
Americana: https://youtu.be/SlPrqwwiaOY
High Percentage Americana: https://youtu.be/VOiFJf8VrZI

Josh Barnett Americana: https://youtu.be/g1eSGYM0QbQ
Americana and Kimura: https://youtu.be/vjNXcnmZ7wg

6. Armbar

When you apply the Inverse Armbar you trap your opponent's wrist between your own head and shoulder and apply pressure onto his elbow using your arms. This submission is normally accompanied by a knee mount or a close guard position.

How to execute this move:

a) Get your opponent in a closed guard position.

b) Secure the right sleeve of your opponent with your left hand. Cross grab their right elbow with your right hand. As you grab the arm, lift your hips off the floor to apply more power into the arm pulling process.

c) Pull their arm over and secure their chest and legs. Meanwhile open both legs and through them upwards in a crossing manner.

d) Immediately close your legs and lock your opponent's shoulder up to keep them from getting away.

e) Squeeze both knees to one side and cross your opponent's face with their hand so that they become defensless.

f) Place your left leg over your opponent's face and pull your hips upwards while controlling the arm. The technique is complete and your opponent must submit.

Video of Armbar:
Ronda Rousey Armbar: https://youtu.be/3lXdVDJxDg4
10 ways to finish the Armbar: https://youtu.be/8wNQ5UGLQHk
Armbar from Mount: https://youtu.be/ECPcvbKt-lY

7. Omoplata

The omoplata comes from the Greek word «ωμοπλάτη» which means scapula. The technique can force your opponent to tap out, however depending on their response, you can either incapacitate and get the submission, or achieve a favorable position for other submission techniques (such as taking the back and getting a rear naked choke).

How to execute the technique:

a) Execute an 'armbar' technique against your opponent from the guard position.

b) If your opponent manages to get away from your arm grip, raise your hips and open your knees to keep them from getting away altogether. Use your right hand to add more pressure and twist your opponent's left arm to one side.

c) Bring your right hand to your opponent's belt and your left hand to their trousers. Lock your legs in a figure four position around your opponent's shoulder to get yourself into position.

d) To defend thesmelves, your opponent will probably turn into you by raising their head. Open your legs and keep your hips high to maintain your position.

e) Place your right foot onto your opponent's left hip and kick your left leg over the back of his neck while pulling his arm toward you.

f) To get the submission, close your legs in the triangle position, lift your hips and choke the head.

Video of Omoplatas:
Omoplata: https://youtu.be/LVy4tGv5Fk4
4 ways to Improve your omoplata: https://youtu.be/5mwTslcGH1Y

8. Gogoplata

The Gogoplata is a variation of the Omoplata technique for flexible fighters. To apply it you weave the foot that traps your opponent's arm around their throat, then press the foot into the throat to complete the choke.

How to execute the technique:

a) Drop your opponent to the floor, and bring him in the guard position on top of your body.

b) Grab your opponent's hand or arm that is parallel to your right arm and pull it toward your left shoulder.

c) As you force the arm put your right leg under your jaw, so that your shin and lower leg is against your opponent's neck or throat.

d) Bring the opponent's arm that you grabbed in step 2 to the area of your abdomen and release it.

e) Place your left leg against your opponent's neck so that your legs form an "h".

f) Put your hands behind your opponent's head and draw it toward your legs.

Videos of the Gogoplata:
Regular Gogoplata: https://youtu.be/uTKDmjU88Jc
No-Gi Gogoplata: https://youtu.be/pFZxBSa1vLY
Gogplata from Mount: https://youtu.be/MnauxGlVm2g

9. Figure 4 Toehold

You may have seen your most favourite wrestling stars performing the figure four leg lock on TV, and now you have decided to attempt it yourself. This move can be an awesome approach in the battle with your opponent, yet it is important that it is executed correctly. Keep reading so that you may learn how to do so.

How to execute the technique:

a) First of all, make sure that your opponent is lying flat on the ground before you can begin executing the technique.

b) Grab his right leg and put your left leg over it, so that you are facing away from your opponent.

c) Then grab their left leg and bend the other one until their right foot rests on their left leg over the knee. Face to one side of your opponent. At this point your opponent's legs should be forming a kind of a "P", or a "4" shape with your right leg forming the tail of it.

d) Hold that position and fall back. You'll need to twist a bit in the right, so that you can lay on your back. Make sure that you are at the opposite side of your opponent and not facing him.

e) To complete the technique, take your left leg and place it over your opponent's foot.

f) If is possible to modify the technique and execute it in reverse. The difference in this variation is that you need to make your opponent lay on their back and place their left leg underneath your thigh.

g) Then push their right leg up hard until their left foot comes beneath their thigh. Keep pushing forward but not too hard.

Videos of the toehold:
Toehold: https://youtu.be/o8jrAKnGqnw
Basic Toehold: https://youtu.be/1lYsi1Y-rGY
Toehold Variation: https://youtu.be/mFno2NYeaJI
Toehold to tap Larger Opponents: https://youtu.be/hLef63326MA

Not all of the above techniques are legitimate for execution in a competition. However, they are permitted and taught in all gyms. Legitimacy aside, you should be familiar with these illegal texhniques should the case be that someone tries to use them on you.

Another reason to learn the aforementioned techniques is that they are still valid as far as self defense is concerned and for various MMA applications. Just make sure they are properly and well executed.

The Different Guards of Mixed Martial Arts

The guard is a grappling position on the ground in which one combatant has their back to the ground while attempting to control the other combatant using their legs. In grappling combat martial arts, the guard is considered an advantageous position, because the bottom combatant can attack with various joint locks and chokeholds, while the combatant on top's priority is to transition into a more dominant position, known as passing the guard.

In MMA (Mixed Martial Arts) competition or hand-to-hand combat in general, it is possible to effectively strike from the top in the guard, even though the bottom combatant exerts some control. There are various types of guard, with their own advantages and disadvantages.

The guard is a key part of MMA (BJJ) where it can be used as an offensive position. It is also used, but not formally named, in judo though it is sometimes referred to as "do-osae" in Japanese, meaning "trunk hold". It is called the "front body scissor" in catch wrestling.

Pulling Guard

Pulling guard is so common place in MMA that you see it in almost every competition video known to man. I have seen with the high level grapplers like Rousimar Palhares all the way down to children in their first ever competition.

However, I have seen it time-and-time again where someone pulls guard and just doesn't know what to do from there. Willingly pulling guard means that you have to be aggressive enough to work from this position, and not just sit there like a fish out of water.

When you should pull guard:

- Your opponent is a high level wrestler, or a Judo black belt.
- Your opponent is much bigger than you.
- You are injured and cannot fight on your feet.
- Strategy: your guard is much better than your top game.

Closed Guard

The closed guard is sometimes referred to as the full guard. The closed guard is the typical guard position. The legs are hooked behind the back of the opponent, preventing them from standing up or moving away. The opponent needs to open the legs up to be able to improve positioning. The bottom combatant might transition between the open and closed guard, as the open guard allows for better movement, but also there's an increased risk of the opponent passing the guard.

Open Guard

The open guard is typically used to perform various joint locks and chokeholds. The legs can be used to move the opponent, and to create leverage. The legs open allows the opponent to stand up or try to pass the guard, so this position is often used temporarily to set up sweeps or other techniques. Open guard is also a general term that encompasses a large number of guard positions where the legs are used to push, wrap or hook the opponent without locking the ankles together around them.

Butterfly Guard

The butterfly guard or hooks guard, in Portuguese: guarda de gancho(s) or guarda borboleta, is one of the oldest and most traditional forms of guard playing in jiu jitsu and is often labelled as a classic guard. The butterfly hooks are designed to jeopardize the base of the fighter with the top position (this being defined by the hind end off the ground and in most cases head above that of the guard player) using the bottom player's feet as hooks against the inside of the guard passer's legs.

The Butterfly Guard allows you to quickly attack your opponent with sweeps and transitions. The Butterfly Guard will also allow you to defeat a much larger and stronger opponent.

We will look at how to maintain the Butterfly Guard and how to attack from this unique position.

In some BJJ circles, the Butterfly Guard is sometimes called Seated Guard because you are sitting up right as you try to launch your attacks.

Many people attempt to be offensive with their Butterfly Guard once they are on their backs. This is a very dangerous mistake.

Unless you quickly transition to Half Guard or X Guard, you will probably get your Guard passed quickly.

It is much easier for your training partner to pass your Butterfly Guard once your shoulder blades are down on the mat.

Remember, the Butterfly Guard is only offensive if you are sitting up. With the shoulder blades off the ground and sitting up like you are sitting at the beach.

It is extremely difficult to initiate a Sweep or a Submission from the Butterfly Guard once your shoulder blades are down on the mat.

Often, when BJJ practitioners play the Butterfly Guard, they'll keep their feet on the mat and think that their knees and shins will keep them safe from the Guard Pass.

This is foolhardy and most people will find themselves in bottom cross side very quickly.

The correct way to use your feet is to have them glued to your training partner's legs.

At least one foot is touching your training partner's legs at all times. This does take awareness, sensitivity and practice, but it will make your Butterfly Guard much more difficult to pass.

From the Butterfly Guard, the most immediate attack from this position is to sweep your opponent.

When attempting a Butterfly Guard Sweep, many people will keep both feet glued to the inside of their training partner's legs.

Although this is a good tactic initially, one foot needs to be placed on the mat to help apply leverage for the sweep as the other foot lifts your training partner up for the sweep.

The foot that is placed on the mat has to be in a very specific spot: just outside of your training partner's knee.

The moment you go for the sweep, if you have both your feet in between your training partner's legs, you need to bring your right foot underneath your left knee so that it will rest against the outside of your training partner's right knee.

Many people see the Butterfly Guard Sweep as a sweep done with one leg.

They'll keep one leg on the mat while the other leg elevates their opponent; but, if their opponent has good balance and tries to defend the sweep, then the sweep is quickly nullified.

What you need to do is think of the Butterfly Guard Sweep as a 2 legged sweep – one leg elevates your training partner and the second leg drives aggressively into the mat. Doing the sweep this way is far more effective.

X-Guard

The x-guard is an open guard where one of the combatants is standing up and the other is on their back. The bottom combatant uses the legs to entangle one of the opponent's legs, which creates opportunities for powerful sweeps. The x-guard is often used in combination with butterfly and half guard. In a grappling match, this is an advantageous position for the bottom combatant, but in general hand-to-hand combat, the top combatant can attack with stomps or soccer kicks. Likewise, skilled use of the x-guard can prevent the opponent from attempting a kick, or throw them off balance should they raise a leg. The x-guard was popularised by Marcelo Garcia.

Spider Guard

The spider guard comprises a number of positions, all of which involve controlling the opponent's arms while using the soles of the feet to control the opponent at the biceps, hips, thighs, or a combination of them. It is most effective when the sleeves of the opponent can be grabbed, for instance if the opponent is wearing a gi. The spider guard can be used for sweeps and to set-up joint locks or chokeholds.

De la Riva Guard

The De la Riva guard (also called the De la Riva hook and Jello guard) is an open guard that was popularized in BJJ by black belt Ricardo de la Riva Goded, who was successful with it in competition. In it, one of the legs is wrapped behind the opponent's leg from the outside, the ankle held with one hand, and the other hand grips one of their sleeves. The De la Riva guard offers many sweeps, transitions and submissions, and is often used in combination with the spider guard.

Rubber Guard

The rubber guard is a grappling position of unknown origin that was first seen being put to use in competitions by Nino Schembri in the late 1990s, later being also picked up by Eddie Bravo in the early 2000s, who developed a training method heavily based on this particular situation. The rubber guard is a variation of the open guard where the guard player will grab his own shin with the opposite arm (example: right arm grabbing left shin) over his opponent's back, the grip should be performed with the palm of the hand facing upwards and the forearm should be in contact with the collarbone. These details will help the guard player keep his opponent's posture down, avoiding this way for the guard passer to pose an offence.

In MMA, and despite the position's main aim of helping Jiu Jitsu succeed in this environment, it seems to have fallen into a limbo. As the UFC evolved to shorter rounds with a scoring system that benefits striking, takedowns and top control on the ground, the rubber guard's efficiency in the sport was compromised, as it too often relies on time to work the top fighter into a submission.

50/50 Guard (Fifty – Fifty Guard)

The 50-50 (Fifty-fifty) guard is a position popularized by Roberto "Gordo" Correa and extensively used by the Mendes Brothers, Rafael and Guilherme Mendes, Bruno Frazzato, Ryan Hall and Ramon Lemos from the Atos Jiu-Jitsu Team. In other grappling systems such as catch wrestling and Russian Sambo, it is a form of the "outside leg triangle" type of leg control. In this position, the fighter on the bottom crosses a triangle on the opponent's leg, which allows for the leg to be dominated while leaving the arms free to work on sweeps and submissions. This position has been heavily criticized for use in competitions with restricted use of leglocks due to the potential of stalling a match when the fighter on top cannot pass the guard and the fighter on the bottom cannot successfully perform a sweep.

Preparing for your first MMA Fight

Your very first Mixed Martial Arts fight is one of the most exhilarating, confusing and truly scary experiences that you will face in your entire life. People often say they respect anyone that that has the balls to step into a cage and that sentiment is echoed for good reason. You are entering a locked arena where only one of you is going to come out the other side as the winner. In a combat sport based on pure competition such as MMA, winning is the ultimate goal.

Let's be honest, winning your first fight is not that important. You would be surprised how many professional UFC fighters lost their first professional bouts.

If it is only an amateur bout, it's even less important. Every fight you take part in feels like the most important moment of your life. But realise that winning or losing is secondary to the experience you gain from fighting. You may well be terrified at the prospect of your first fight so here is some advice for amateur fighters making their Mixed Martial Arts debut.

Keep Calm – or try your best to

Nerves are a double edged sword in Mixed Martial Arts. Going into your first MMA fight, the adrenaline rush you get is almost impossible to describe. Everything about it will feel new (and unknown) and that adds to the nervousness you will feel. Rest assured even the most battle hardened veterans among MMA fighters get nervous for fights. UFC fighter Georges St. Pierre is famous for feeling scared before fights. Even after all this time he openly admits that he still feels terrified before a fight.

The key to success is to manage those nerves accordingly. If you go in to the fight too calm, you may be overwhelmed by a more eager opponent. But be too nervous, and you'll make mistakes that they can capitalise on.

Realise that you aren't made of glass

A rule I feel I should have told myself before my first fight. I was so afraid of being KO'd or having something broken that I almost ran out of the venue before my fight. But as time, experience and sparring have taught me, no matter how small you are. We can all take a bit of a beating. Obviously, I don't advocate getting beaten up. But remembering you can take a punch gives you a bit of fire to back yourself up.

Pick a great entrance song that evokes something in you

I always walk out to the same track 'My Own Summer' by Deftones. When I had my debut fight, this was the song that filled me with adrenaline. Afterwards, despite falling out of love with Deftones, the track was permanently etched as my 'fight-mode' song.

Entrance music should exhilarate you, or mean something. Music is a motivator proven by the success of musical fitness classes all over the world over. A good song gets you in the right mood and in some ways gives you comfort and familiarity as you walk into the alien cage.

Consider your opponent – he is probably just as scared as you

If you fight someone who is also making their MMA debut, you have to remember you are on an even keel. In my first fight I recall being intimidated by my opponent's shorter yet bulkier frame and the fact he looked a lot older than me. However, I can bet in hindsight that he was just as scared as I was. Luckily I won that fight, but it's important to remember that no matter how scary they look to you, they are probably just as nervous inside. Remember, looks don't win fights good technique does.

Enjoy it

Remembering to enjoy the experience is the single greatest piece of advice I can think of. Your first MMA fight is an important event that, win or lose, helps define you as a person.

My fight went well and I won in the first round, but it was more the fact I even stepped into a cage to fight another human being that I take pride in. The rush of the crowd, the searing heat of the lighting over the cage, the wild yet controlled chaos of the fight – all of these things happen so fast and then are suddenly over.

Your debut will come and go, making you doubt why you spent all of those weeks worrying or debating what it would be like. No matter what the outcome, the most important thing to take away is that you have done something that less than 1% of the population would ever dare to do. You have done it (or if you're reading this before a fight – you will do it). For that, I applaud you. Never forget your first fight. It's a defining moment, a learning experience and a damn good way to find out just how much you love competition.

Cutting weight for your first MMA fight

The following is how Georges St Pierre cuts weight for his fights. I personally think you should cut weight by dieting especially if you are fighting at the amateur level. As always consult with your coaches and nutritionists before attempting any weight cuts yourself. Dehydrating yourself is dangerous and can be fatal if done incorrectly.

Done right a weight cut can significantly increase a fighter's chances of winning. An athlete will artificially lower his/her weight for pre-fight weigh-ins, then show up to the actual fight 10, 20, or even 30 pounds heavier than their opponent. It can be a game changer.

Done incorrectly, it can make even the toughest guy lose his edge and probably the fight. There is also a serious risk of organ failure if done haphazardly.

Even though professional boxers and wrestlers have been manipulating weight in this fashion for decades, it has the air of illicit behaviour. And although it's legal in MMA competition, you should NEVER try this at home or without medical supervision. Excessive dehydration can kill you. "Cutting weight" has no place in real-world dieting or behaviour.

It is Saturday night and you are a top ranked MMA fighter who just stepped into the cage to fight for the 170 pound Welterweight Championship.

How much do you weigh?

The answer may seem obvious: 170 pounds? But if you followed the steps of cutting wieght, the real answer is that you weigh somewhere between 185 and 190 pounds. That's 15 to 20 pounds *more* than the "cut-off" weight of 170.

24 hours *before* you stepped into the cage, however, you did in fact weigh 170 pounds. Friday night was the official weigh-in where you and your opponent stripped down to your

underwear, stepped on the scale in front of the judge, and prayed that the number on the scale hit 170 or lower.

As soon as you stepped off it was a race to gain the weight back again.

Most regular guys have a hard time gaining or losing just five pounds at a time.

But the top combat athletes can lose up to 30 pounds in just *5 days* leading up to the fight. Then they can gain nearly all of it back again in the 24 hours between weighing in and the fight.

They do this to gain a massive competitive advantage. In other words, the bigger guy who retains more of his strength, agility, and endurance will have a huge advantage and likely win. The guy who weighs in at 170, and then *fights* at 170, often has a world of hurt coming at him (unless he is called Frankie Edgar or BJ Penn).

GSP normally walks around at 195 pounds and cuts the 25 pounds to make it down to his 170 pound weight class. He then gains 20 pounds of it back before he fights.

Cutting weight like a pro

Now extreme weight cutting can go horribly wrong. Even a lot of UFC guys don't know how to do it properly. Instead they put their bodies in real harm by doing stupid things like taking a lot of diuretics, not drinking any water, missing meals, wearing trash bags while exercising (sometimes even inside the sauna!) and generally being idiotic.

They will lose the weight of course but they also lose power and energy in the process not to mention they run the risk of serious harm.

Carefully decrease water consumption

Dropping the weight fast is all about carefully manipulating your water and sodium levels.

For an MMA fighter who wants to cut weight quickly and safely, here's how much water he would consume in the five days leading up to his weigh in.

Sunday – 2 gallons
Monday – 1 gallon
Tuesday – 1 gallon
Wednesday – .5 gallons
Thursday – .25 gallons
Friday – No water till after weigh-in at 5PM.

As you can see, the amount of water starts high with a full two gallons and decreases with each day until he's drinking hardly any water on Thursday and Friday.

This is to ensure their body gets into a "flushing mode."

By drinking a lot of water early on, the fighter's body will down regulate *aldosterone* a hormone that acts to conserve sodium and secrete potassium.

And when the fighter suddenly reduces the amount of water he drinks in the middle and end of the week, his body will still be in flushing mode, meaning he will still run to the bathroom to pee a lot even though he's hardly drinking any water.

What happens when you excrete more fluid than you take in? You get rapid weight loss.

DO NOT EAT MORE THAN 50 GRAMS OF CARBS PER DAY

Since one gram of carbohydrate pulls in 2.7 grams of water into the body it's important for fighters to keep their carb intake low.

By doing this the fighter also depletes muscle glycogen (a source of energy) and keeps their body in "flush mode".

DON'T EAT FRUIT, SUGAR, OR STARCHES

These are carbs that should be avoided entirely while cutting.

EAT MEALS THAT CONTAIN A LOT OF PROTEIN AND FAT

MMA Fighters have to eat *something*. Since they are avoiding carbs Dr Berardi advises them to load up on high-quality protein like meats, eggs or vegetarian sources of protein.

It's also the perfect opportunity to eat lots of leafy vegetables (like spinach) and cruciferous vegetables (like broccoli and cauliflower).

GSP normally has his meals prepared by a private chef so he doesn't even have to think about this stuff or make decisions.

DON'T EAT SALT

Since the body likes to hold on to sodium (which will in turn hold on to water) dropping salt helps the fighter's body flush water out.

CONSIDER A NATURAL DIURETIC

This step is not always necessary, but it can help as a last resort when you're close to the weigh ins and still need to lose water. Opt for a natural diuretic like dandelion root, but wait until the last two days to use it.

TAKE HOT BATHS

We sweat a lot in hot environments. However, we sweat the most in hot, humid environments. Since hot water offers both heat and 100% humidity, MMA fighters lose water quickly by taking hot baths and fully submerging everything but their nose for 5 to 10 minutes at a time.

SIT IN THE SAUNA

This is the finishing touch to flush the last few pounds of water and is only used on the last few days leading up to the weigh-in.

The weight cutting schedule

So if we take all of that and break it into a weekly plan, it looks like this:

SUNDAY
Carbs: Less than 50 grams per day. No fruit, starches, or sugars.
Protein and Fat: As much as you want in 3 meals
Water: 2 gallons
Salt: None

MONDAY
Carbs: Less than 50 grams per day. No fruit, starches, or sugars.
Protein and Fat: As much as you want in 3 meals
Water: 1 gallon
Salt: None

TUESDAY
Carbs: Less than 50 grams per day. No fruit, starches, or sugars.
Protein and Fat: As much as you want in 3 meals
Water: 1 gallon
Salt: None

WEDNESDAY
Carbs: Less than 50 grams per day. No fruit, starches, or sugars.
Protein and Fat: As much as you want in 3 meals
Water: 0.5 gallon

Salt: None
Sauna in afternoon

THURSDAY
Carbs: Less than 50 grams per day. No fruit, starches, or sugars.
Protein and Fat: As much as you want in 3 meals
Water: 0.25 gallon
Salt: None
Sauna in afternoon for 30 minutes, hot water bath at night

FRIDAY (WEIGH IN AT 6PM)
Carbs: Less than 50 grams per day. No fruit, starches, or sugars.
Protein and Fat: Eat 2 very small meals until weigh in
Water: None until weigh in
Salt: None
Sauna until weight is met

Putting the weight back on again

Once the MMA fighters cut weight and weigh-in, they'd never be able to perform at the top level.

So what do they do next? They gain as much weight as humanly possible in 24 hours.

Here's how to do it.

DRAMATICALLY INCREASE WATER INTAKE.
The body can absorb only about 1 liter (2.2 pounds) of fluid at maximum in an hour. So do not to drink any more than that. Instead sip 1 liter (2.2 pounds) of water per hour.

However, the fighters won't retain all that fluid. In fact, probably about 25% of it will be lost as pee.

So, here's the math for someone like GSP:

- 9 liters (20 pounds) of water to get most of the weight back.
- 11 liters (25 pounds) of fluid between Friday weigh-in and Saturday weigh-in to get all the weight back.
- 24 hours in which to do it, 8 of which he will be asleep and 3 of which will be leading up to Saturday weigh-in.

This leaves 13 total hours for rehydration.

So as soon as GSP steps off the scale, he literally slams a liter of water and carries the bottle around with him, refilling it and draining it every hour until 3 hours before his fight.

EAT AS MUCH CARBOHYDRATES (AND PROTEIN AND FAT) AS YOU LIKE

Now is the time for fighters to load up on carbs and pull all the water they are drinking back into their muscles. It also helps them feel more human and look less sickly.

Eat a big meal directly after the weigh in. Do not restrict calories. You can eat as much as you want in that meal as long as it is healthy food like lean meats, sweet potatoes, rice, and vegetables. Stuffing your face with junk food is a very bad idea as it will make you sluggish.

Then on Saturday (the day of the fight), eat a satisfying amount of healthy food in a few small meals leading up to the fight.

ADD SALT TO EVERYTHING

Since sodium helps the body retain water, you are encouraged to add extra salt to your meals.

Putting the weight back on again

FRIDAY AFTER WEIGH-IN

Carbs: Eat as much as you want in one meal after weigh-in and testing
Protein and Fat: Eat as much as you want in one meal after weigh-in and testing
Rehydration Beverage: Drink 1 liter of water mixed with 1/2 scoop of carbohydrate/protein drink for every hour you're awake
Salt: Salt your food

SATURDAY
Carbs: Eat satisfying amount in the four meals before the fight
Protein: Eat satisfying amount in four meals before the fight
Rehydration Beverage: Drink 1 liter of water mixed with 1/2 scoop of carbohydrate/protein drink for every hour you're awake.

Do you have a fight coming up and you need to drop some weight? Here is how to quickly shed pounds with this two week diet meal plan. As always I recommend you consult your coach and team before chaging your diet and get their thoughts on it.

I do not recommend that anyone follows this meal plan for more than two weeks.

As a fighter, you will not continue to see results with this kind of extreme diet.

These example dietary suggestions are mainly for Mixed Martial Arts fighters that need to drop 8-15 pounds in order to make weight.

I do not recommend that you wait until the last minute to start dropping weight because it is not safe. Plus the weight can easily come back.

Fighters will however try anything, even when they are fully aware of the dangers. I've heard all sorts of crazy stories, one starved himself for almost two weeks. Another only drank lemon water, while another onyl ate two bananas and protein.

All of these can be very dangerous. I would not design a nutrition plan like that for anyone else. It is merely a quick way to loose weight while preserving as much muscle as possible. The reality is when you go on a crazy diet that makes you loose weight rapidly you will lose muscle mass along with fat.

While you are dropping weight quickly you will need to taper down on your training significantly. Otherwise this will not work. When you drastically reduce your daily calorie intake, your training can suffer since you won't be properly fueled for the grueling workouts. Use this time to train lightly while focusing on the easiest way to shed the weight. Bear in mind that the first few pounds that come off will most likely be water weight; the rest will be fat and some muscle.

For the next fortnight, focus most of your meals on high-quality, lean protein such as fish, eggs, chicken, turkey, or Greek Yogurt. Because you need to reduce your calories, you will need to go for the lower fat items. Rather than three whole eggs, take out at least two of the yolks in order to lower the calorie content. Since Mixed Martial Arts fighters along with most people live on the go and don't always have time to cook, protein powders are allowed but should only be used right before or after a workout.

Eat lots of vegetables

Eating higher fiber vegetables will allow you to feel fuller and more satisfied for a longer period of time. Always having a bunch of vegetables on hand is an amazing way to keep your hunger at bay between meals. For this plan, you will want to make sure that you are not stocking up on the starchy vegetables (such as potatoes), but focusing more on eating the highly fibrous ones; e.g. cucumber, spinach, celery, red peppers, asparagus, broccoli, zucchini and cabbage.

A few other things to keep in mind:

You will want to make sure to eat a small amount of fat. You can take a fish oil or a DHA supplement throughout this period. In the sample meal plan, I will include some natural, healthy fat sources that will not hinder your weight loss goal. Fat will be the one thing that you really want to measure out on this program. When eating lots of salads, it is very easy to pile on the oils which can cause weight gain.

It is important to measure portions throughout your diet.

Drink a lot of water

When reducing your carbohydrates to this low amount, you will lose a lot of water (through going to the bathroom more) as well as important electrolytes. Drinking clean water on a regular basis is a must. You can add fresh squeezed lemon or just a touch of pink salt to each liter in order to add back the magnesium you are losing. You can add some pink salt (lightly) to your vegetables as well, just not too much.

I am a huge fan of fruit because they contain so many vitamins and minerals. For this particular diet however you will not be eating them often. Fruit will mainly be your sugar source right before and/or after a workout to aid recovery. THAT WILL BE IT! If you feel that you are going to fall off the wagon and develop a crazy sweet tooth, then I suggest that you eat apples, pears, and bananas as opposed to ice cream or cookies, but remember this is for only two weeks. Suck it up and you will get your reward during or after your MMA fight.

Depending on your start weight and how much you have to lose, you can tailor these ideas so that they fit your specific goals. If you are a very large male (Heavyweight, Light Heavyweight), then you may need much more than what I have written down here. On the other hand, if you are a tiny female (Strawweight), then you may need only half as much. Here is a sample day with a scheduled morning workout.

Example Day Meals

Wake Up

- 16oz Water with Lemon

Breakfast (Pre-Workout)

- Green Protein Smoothie

- 1-2 cups Spinach, 1 banana, 1 serving of Grass Fed Whey, Sprouted Brown Rice or Pea protein powder, blended with ice and water)

- 1 teaspoon of Fish Oil taken separately

Post Workout

- Organic Plain Nonfat Greek Yogurt

- 2 Tbs of Chopped Walnuts

- 1/2 cup Organic Blueberries

Lunch

- Large Green Salad made up of 1 cup Baby Romaine, 1 cup of Spinach, 1 cup of Cabbage topped with Cucumbers, Tomatoes, Mushrooms

- Protein can be mixed in. 1 Can of Wild River Tuna. Just tossed with vinegar, mustard, green onions and celery.

- Dressing for salad can be LIGHTLY tossed with Olive Oil, lemon, and vinegar.

Snack

- 1-2 Red Peppers and 1 Sliced Cucumber

- 3 Hard Boiled eggs with 1 yolk

Dinner

- 1 bunch of Grilled Asparagus and Zucchini lightly tossed in Olive Oil and Himalayan Pink Salt

- 3-4 oz of Organic Chicken or Turkey grilled, baked, or slow cooked.

- 1/2 cup Organic Low Sodium black beans topped with Pico De Gallo

Evening Snack (Only if hungry)

- 2oz of Organic Chicken or Turkey

- Sliced cucumbers and celery

Get as creative as you like with this program. Always remember to drink lots of fresh water throughout the day. If you end up doing a very hard work out while on this diet, then you might want to sip on coconut water. Stick to the main concept of low starchy carbohydrates, lots of vegetables, and lean proteins, along with some fruit and small amounts of healthy fat, and you will see amazing results.

Common MMA Gym Terms

Here is a collection of common Mixed Martial Arts terms that you will usually hear in gym so you can understand what they all mean.

Arm Bar: An arm bar is a submission hold where a fighter puts pressure on his/her opponent's elbow joint by attempting to bend it the way it does not naturally bend. The competitor positions himself so that the opponent's arm is between his legs, enabling him to use his hips to leverage the pressure.

Axe Kick: A kick executed by a standing MMA fighter, frequently against an opponent who is on the ground, usually referred to as a downed opponent. The standing fighter raises one leg straight in the air and brings it straight down, like the motion of someone swinging an axe to chop wood. It is usually the heel that makes contact with the opponent.

Back Control: Also known as taking someone's back. This is a position where one fighter gets behind the other and controls him by wrapping his legs around the back of the opponent and placing his heels (also known as "hooks") inside the opponent's thighs, also while controlling the torso and arms from the back. Having back control is considered to be a very advantageous position. This is because the person who is being controlled cannot defend well, especially if the person with control is on top of the other person, both people face down. Also the person on the back usually can't be hit or submitted.

Choke: The choke is a finishing hold that cuts off the blood and/or the oxygen to a MMA fighter's brain. A player who does not tap to a well-executed choke will pass out. There are different kinds of chokes, some that use the forearms or biceps to put pressure on the arteries in the neck and/or the windpipe, and others that use the legs around the head and arm. There are two types of choke; the blood choke that cuts off circulation and an air choke which restricts air flow in the wind pipe to make breathing difficult.

Clinch: The clinch is a position where competitors try to control each other's bodies by wrapping their arms around one another, fighting for good arm and hip position, frequently as a precursor to a takedown attempt of throwing some knee strikes.

Cross: A cross is a punch frequently used in combination with the jab and executed with the non-jabbing arm. The cross normally packs more power than a jab.

Dirty Boxing: Dirty boxing is a combination of wrestling and boxing techniques that enables a competitor to close the distance between himself and his opponent and execute punches and elbows from the clinch. Randy Couture was a great example of this style.

Elbow Strike or Elbow: This is a blow to the opponent's body or head using the point of the elbow. Elbow strikes are very painful, and they can also open cuts. The use of elbows is generally heavily regulated. For instance, a competitor may not raise his elbow straight in the air and bring it straight down upon his opponent (known as a 12-6 elbow). Elbows must come in at an angle for safety.

Ground and Pound: A strategy where a competitor takes his opponent to the ground with a takedown and unleashes a flurry of punches and elbows to try to finish a fight. Mark Coleman is a good example of this style.

Guard: The guard is a BJJ/grappling position where one player is on his back and has his legs around an opponent, who is either standing up or kneeling. A competitor who is in someone's guard may try to pass the guard and get to side control or the mount, both of which are more offensive positions, though the competitor may also try to land blows from the guard. A competitor who has someone in his guard wants to prevent his opponent from passing, and avoid getting punched or kicked. The competitor who has someone in his guard can also set up submissions such as triangles, guillotine chokes and kimuras.

Guillotine: The guillotine is a choke a fighter executes by positioning himself in front of his opponent, wrapping his arm around the top of the opponent's neck and under the chin, and applying pressure on the neck and throat. The guillotine can place a lot of pressure on the neck as well as render an opponent unconscious. It can also be turned into a neck crank if the opponent does not tap.

Hammerfist: A hammerfist is a type of punch where the competitor brings the bottom (pinky side) of his closed fist into contact with his opponent with speed and as much force as possible. This was Brock Lesnar's favourite technique.

Hook: The hook is a punch where the fighter cocks his arm at a 90-degree angle in front of his body with the force coming from the side rather than straight on or from underneath. Not to be confused with the hooks when taking the back in grappling.

Hooks: The hooks are a technique of using the feet, specifically when a competitor takes an opponent's back and has anchored his heels around his opponent's legs. The act of getting one's heels around one's opponent's legs is called "putting in your hooks."

Jab: The jab is a straight punch using the hand that is closest to the opponent.

Leg Kick: A kick a competitor lands on his opponent's leg. Multiple leg kicks can cause accumulated damage and fatigue and disrupt an opponent's balance. Fighters can be TKO's from leg kicks if they cannot stand.

Leg Lock: A leg lock is a finishing hold where a competitor isolates part of the opponent's leg or foot to put pressure on the knee, ankle, or toes. The pressure from some leg locks such as the kneebar or heel hook can come on quickly, and frequently by the time the recipient feels pain from these leg locks, the damage has already been done to the knee joint or ankle.

Mount: The Mount is a ground position where a competitor is on top of his opponent with his legs around the opponent's body. The opponent is on his back, and the competitor is facing him, driving his hips forward to maintain pressure. People who are competing may "go to mount" or may "get mounted." This position is very advantageous for the person on top and very dangerous for the person on the bottom. The person on the bottom is susceptible to strikes and from getting submitted.

Rear Naked Choke: The rear naked choke is a choke hold executed from back control where a competitor wraps one bare arm around the opponent's neck under the chin (hence the naked) and reinforces that grip with the other arm to force a tap out.

Side Control: Side control (also known as side mount) is a position where a competitor immobilizes an opponent by lying perpendicularly across the other player who is on his/her back or side, controlling the head and hips.

Spinning Back-Fist: The spinning back fist is a punch where a competitor starts out facing his opponent and then spins around quickly with one fist outstretched, using the momentum generated from the spin to put force behind the resulting strike.

Spinning Back-Kick: The Spinning Back Kick is a kick executed in a manner similar to the above spinning back-fist.

Sprawl: A sprawl is a reaction to a takedown attempt, where the competitor jumps back, drops his/her hips, and drives their weight into the opponent who is attempting to take them down.

Superman: This is a punch where a competitor fakes a front kick and then draws the kicking leg back quickly, while simultaneously throwing a punch with the same side fist. The force of the kick is transferred to the punch, and the supporting foot leaves the ground to deliver a powerful strike.

Sweep: A sweep is a move where a competitor who has an opponent in the guard (or half guard) takes away the opponent's balance, turns him over, and ends up on top, frequently in the mount or side control. Sweeps are dependent upon the sweeper's ability to remove all of the opponent's supports on one side known as the base, by making it impossible for the opponent to "base out" with a hand or a foot.

Swing for the Fences: This is an expression indicating that competitors are giving it everything and putting it all on the line to try and win the round or the fight (e.g., "He's swinging for the fences to try to get the decision.").

Takedown: The takedown is a method for getting an opponent on the ground and getting on top of him, borrowed heavily from wrestling and Judo. Competitors can "shoot in" for a takedown or attempt one from the clinch.

Tap Out: Tapping out is a way to submit to a finishing hold because it is on securely and the opponent is in pain or in danger of being put to sleep. Competitors who tap out literally tap the mat or the opponent to signal that they want the opponent to stop. This makes the referee step in to end the fight.

Triangle: The triangle choke is performed by a competitor wrapping his/her legs around the opponent's head and one of his arms, bending one knee over the other ankle/shin. Named for the shape of the space between the legs, this kind of choke can be executed from the guard or from the mount.

Uppercut: An uppercut is a punch the MMA fighter executes by bringing the fist up sharply and quickly, into the face or the body of the opponent. It is normally set up by first throwing a Jab or a Hook with the other hand.

Conclusion

The decision to participate in MMA is a difficult one and shouldn't be rushed. You need to consider all the pro's you will receive from entering a life that can literally take you from a "90 pound weakling" to a 90 pound badass. It can also lead to injuries, broken and sprained limbs and the ever dangerous risk of concussions. This should give any potential fighter pause and the question you need to ask, is it worth it? The answer to that question may be found in the degree you choose to participate.

If you want to increase your fitness and your knowledge of self-defense, then absolutely take part in MMA. It is the best for thing for ultimate cross training. If you decide you want to compete, then that is a major life decision and I hope this article gave you some good advice on how to answer that question. The first step is to go out and try it. Then you will know how to find the answers you seek.

Other Books By The Same Author

Brazilian Jiu-Jitsu: The Ultimate Guide to Beginning BJJ

Getting started in Brazilian Jiu-Jitsu can be daunting.

But training martial arts is one of the most beneficial things I've ever done, mentally and physically, but getting over the beginner's hump was where a chunk of those benefits come from.

Thankfully the Internet now allows us to learn more easily from those who came before us

Here is what you will learn in Beginning Brazilian Jiu-Jitsu: The Ultimate Guide

- What is Brazilian Jiu-Jitsu? (An Introduction)
- Why Train BJJ?
- What should I look for in a good BJJ gym
- What happens in a typical BJJ class?
- Is BJJ right for Women?
- How should I wash my gi?
- How often should I train BJJ, as a beginner?
- Is BJJ just a sport, or will it teach me self-defence?
- I'm really out of shape: Do I need to get fitter before starting BJJ?
- What are the belt ranks in BJJ?
- I'm getting frustrated with my lack of progress: how can I overcome this?
- I get tired quickly when sparring: what can I do?
- I'm scared of sparring what should I do?
- How do I avoid injuries in BJJ?

- I'm worried about getting cauliflower ear. How do I avoid it?
- A Guide To Rolling (Sparring)
- A full guide to competing in your first BJJ Competition
- Returning from an Injury
- Why do so many students stop training? And how to stop it from being you
- And much much more

Amazon US Link:
http://www.amazon.com/gp/product/B00V0S0UR0
Amazon UK Link:
http://www.amazon.co.uk/gp/product/B00V0S0UR0

Printed in Great Britain
by Amazon